A Gift for

....

From

....

Date

....

If My People . . .

Published in Nashville, Tennessee, by Thomas Nelson. Thomas Nelson is a registered trademark of HarperCollins Christian Publishing, Inc.

Unless otherwise indicated, Scripture quotations are taken from The New King James Version. © 1982 by Thomas Nelson, Inc. Used by permission. All rights reserved.

Cover Design: Left Coast Design
Interior Design: Kristy Edwards

ISBN-13: 978-1-4002-1970-4

Printed in the United States of America

20 21 22 23 24 POL 5 4 3 2 1

www.thomasnelson.com

If My
PEOPLE

A 40-Day Prayer Guide for Our Nation

JACK COUNTRYMAN

An Imprint of Thomas Nelson Publishers

THOMAS NELSON
Since 1798

FREEDOM IS NEVER FREE

Throughout the history of our country, men and women have been called to make a great sacrifice and give their time—and sometimes their very lives—so that we might enjoy freedom, liberty, and the pursuit of happiness. With every challenge we have faced, we have risen to defend the nation we love and cherish.

Today we find ourselves facing many of the same challenges of our forefathers. We have been at war for many years with those who wish to destroy our land and jeopardize our religious freedom. We find ourselves at a crossroads that will determine the direction of our country's future and the role of Christianity in our nation.

The devoted prayers of all citizens will impact the future direction of our beloved country. Our prayer is that this booklet will draw you closer to our heavenly Father as you commit yourself to pray for our country.

★ ★ GOD BLESS AMERICA! ★ ★

Freedom has its life in the hearts, the actions, the spirit of men and so it must be daily earned and refreshed—else like a flower cut from its life-giving roots, it will wither and die.

—DWIGHT D. EISENHOWER

THE POWER
OF PRAYER

Since our nation's very first days, God's greatest movements in our midst have been fashioned and sustained by prayer, from the signing of our earliest documents, to our triumphs over days of darkness, to the spiritual awakenings that have sustained our faith and resolve over the centuries. Throughout Scripture and throughout our history as a nation, persistent, prevailing, intentional, and never-ending prayer has always brought the presence of God.

How vast are the possibilities when we pray! Prayer is a wonderful power placed by the almighty God into the hands of His saints. When we humbly seek His face in prayer, He is

4

moved to act on our behalf and accomplish His desires for us.

And when we seek God in prayer for our leaders, we impact the very direction our nation will take. This thirty-day prayer journey is designed to help quicken your prayers, to encourage you to seek God's will for our future and continually intercede on behalf of our nation. Prayerfully seek His face every day, believe that your prayers are making a difference, and claim all victory that is and is to come! For there is tremendous power in prayer.

DAY 1

"If My people who are called by My name will humble themselves, and pray and seek My face, and turn from their wicked ways, then I will hear from heaven, and will forgive their sin and heal their land."

2 CHRONICLES 7:14

Father,
We seek Your sovereign blessing on our nation. Forgive us for our shortcomings and for the times when we have failed You. Draw us back to Your love and strengthen us as a nation to serve and honor You in all that we do. May we forever be faithful to the calling that You have given us. We respectfully and humbly give thanks for Your continued blessing.

"Call to Me, and I will answer you, and show you great and mighty things, which you do not know."

JEREMIAH 33:3

Lord,

You have asked us to call to You, with the promise that You will answer when we do. We humbly seek Your guidance for our nation. Give us wisdom so that we will be a people guided by Your Spirit and filled with Your presence. Help us, O Lord, to honor You in word and deed, that we as a people will have Your blessing and favor.

Independence

DAY 3

★
★★

Be anxious for nothing, but in everything by
prayer and supplication, with thanksgiving,
let your requests be made known to God;
and the peace of God, which surpasses all
understanding, will guard your hearts and
minds through Christ Jesus.

PHILIPPIANS 4:6–7

Father,
The worries of each day are ever around us.
Conflict, both within and without, threatens
the peace we so desperately want and seek.
Father, we come to You with open hearts,
seeking Your guidance and being content
with all that You have given us as a nation.
Guard our hearts, O Lord, so that we will be
faithful to You, and let the peace of Your presence surround us each and every day.

*Now it shall come to pass, if you diligently obey
the voice of the LORD your God, to observe
carefully all His commandments which I
command you today, that the LORD your God
will set you high above all nations of the earth.
And all these blessings shall come upon you and
overtake you, because you obey the voice of the
LORD your God: Blessed shall you be in the city,
and blessed shall you be in the country.*

DEUTERONOMY 28:1–3

Father,
Humble our hearts today so that we will hear
Your voice. Help us as a nation to obey Your
voice in all that we say and do. Continue to
bless us, O Lord, and give us a compassionate
and giving heart toward those around us. Hold
us to a higher calling, that we will carefully
observe Your commandments and be a "nation
under God with liberty and justice for all."

Independence

DAY 5

★
★ ★

I know the thoughts that I think toward you,
says the LORD, thoughts of peace and not of evil,
to give you a future and a hope. Then you will
call upon Me and go and pray to Me, and I will
listen to you. And you will seek Me and find Me,
when you search for Me with all your heart.

JEREMIAH 29:11–13

Father,

We know that Your heart's desire for us is to
be at peace with You and with those around
us. Place within our hearts the desire to live
for You and to listen to the leading of Your
Spirit. Let us diligently search for You. Open
our eyes so that we might see what is good,
honorable, and just for this country and for
the well-being of all people.

GEORGE WASHINGTON

O eternal and everlasting God . . . increase my faith in the sweet promises of the gospel; give me repentance from dead works; pardon my wanderings, and direct my thoughts unto Thyself, the God of my salvation; teach me how to live in Thy fear, labor in thy service, and ever to run in the ways of thy commandments; make me always watchful over my heart, that neither the terrors of conscience, the loathing of holy duties, the love of sin, nor an unwillingness to depart this life, may cast me into a spiritual slumber, but daily frame me more and more into the likeness of Thy Son, Jesus Christ, that living in Thy fear, and dying in Thy favor, I may in Thy appointed time attain the resurrection of the just unto eternal life bless my family, friends, and kindred.

—UNDATED PRAYER FROM
WASHINGTON'S PRAYER
JOURNAL, MOUNT VERNON

DAY 6

★

★★

"Go therefore and make disciples of all the nations, baptizing them in the name of the Father and of the Son and of the Holy Spirit, teaching them to observe all things that I have commanded you; and lo, I am with you always, even to the end of the age."

MATTHEW 28:19–20

Lord,

You have commanded us to make disciples of all nations—may we begin within our own hearts! You are the way, the truth, and the life, and we thank You for Your promise to be with us always. Give us sincerity of heart and unfailing courage to spread this good news, whether with our neighbors across the street or with lost souls across the world. We trust in You to work through us—without You we can do nothing!

"If you abide in Me, and My words abide in you, you will ask what you desire, and it shall be done for you. By this My Father is glorified, that you bear much fruit; so you will be My disciples."

JOHN 15:7–8

Lord,

We the people have become self-absorbed and busy with activities that bring temporal value. Help us turn our hearts back to You and Your Word so our nation will bear the fruit of righteousness and be set above all other nations! Strengthen us with the power of Your Spirit in our inner being as we strive to abide in You and to continue in faith, believing that You will do more for us than we could ever imagine.

Independence

DAY 8

★
★★

Confess your trespasses to one another, and
pray for one another, that you may be healed.
The effective, fervent prayer of a righteous man
avails much.

JAMES 5:16

Father,
Give us Your guidance and strength as we
honestly confess our sins to You and to one
another. And give us compassionate hearts as
we pray for each other and our leaders across
the country and the world. Rid us of judg-
ment, condemnation, and pride, and fill us
with a spirit of grace, mercy, and love. Create
in our hearts a fervent desire to pray every day
for Your leadership to reign in our lives.

The sacrifice of the wicked is an abomi-
nation to the LORD,
But the prayer of the upright is His delight.

PROVERBS 15:8

Father,

Your Word says that if we delight ourselves in You, You will give us the desires of our hearts (Psalm 37:4). Please direct our paths in Your ways everlasting so that Your will becomes our desire, so that Your way becomes our delight. Fill us with the power of Your presence and bind us together as a people of one nation under God. And through each day, to You be the glory for all goodness and blessings that come our way.

Independence

DAY 10

★
★ ★

*Rejoice always, pray without ceasing, in
everything give thanks; for this is the will of
God in Christ Jesus for you.*

1 THESSALONIANS 5:16–18

Father,
The joy of the Lord is our strength; therefore,
let us rejoice as a nation and as a people who
have been blessed beyond all that we could
ask or conceive. Let us pray each day for Your
divine guidance, O Lord, and never forget
Your favor. Thank You, Lord, that You wel-
come us to Your throne of grace to receive
Your blessing.

For Our Country

Almighty God, who has given us this good land for our heritage, we humbly beseech Thee that we may always prove ourselves a people mindful of Thy favor and glad to do Thy will. Bless our land with honorable ministry, sound learning, and pure manners. Save us from violence, discord, and confusion, from pride and arrogance, and from every evil way. Defend our liberties, and fashion into one united people the multitude brought hither out of many kindreds and tongues. Endow with Thy spirit of wisdom those to whom in Thy name we entrust the authority of government, that there may be justice and peace at home, and that through obedience to Thy law, we may show forth Thy praise among the nations of the earth. In time of prosperity, fill our hearts with thankfulness, and in the day of trouble, suffer not our trust in Thee to fail; all of which we ask through Jesus Christ our Lord. Amen.

—1928 UNITED STATES
Book of Common Prayer

DAY 11

The Spirit also helps in our weaknesses. For we do not know what we should pray for as we ought, but the Spirit Himself makes intercession for us with groanings which cannot be uttered.

ROMANS 8:26

Lord,

Thank You, Father, for the gift of Your Spirit who continually helps us overcome our weaknesses. We confess that all things are possible through You and *nothing* is possible without You! Open our hearts and intercede with the Father that we may humble ourselves in Your presence. We thank You for Your forgiveness. Strengthen us to live with purpose and empower us to serve You.

★
★ ★

The LORD is my rock and my fortress and my
*   deliverer;*
My God, my strength, in whom I will trust;
My shield and the horn of my salvation, my
*   stronghold.*
I will call upon the LORD, who is worthy to be
*   praised;*
So shall I be saved from my enemies.

PSALM 18:2–3

Lord,
You are the Rock and Strength of this nation.
You are the only One who can deliver us
from our enemies. We trust in You and pray
humbly for Your guidance and direction for
this great nation. Give us wisdom to make the
right choices. Help us live in such a way that
Your name will be honored in all things. May
You forever be praised.

Independence

DAY 13

Evening and morning and at noon
I will pray, and cry aloud,
And He shall hear my voice.

PSALM 55:17

Father,
We exalt our praise and adoration to You all throughout the day and night! May we never forget that You are merciful and gracious, and that You, our Creator, receive our devotion and prayers with an attentive, listening ear. Give us eyes to see the splendor of Your holiness and ears to hear the majesty of Your voice as You lead us to holy and righteous living.

★
★★

We give thanks to the God and Father of our
Lord Jesus Christ, praying always for you, since
we heard of your faith in Christ Jesus and of
your love for all the saints.

COLOSSIANS 1:3–4

Father,
We humbly come before You and ask that
Your Spirit reach across the lands to all who
are hurting and spiritually lost. Restore their
hearts with hope everlasting; comfort them
with Your tender, loving arms. May we be
sensitive to their needs, whether physical or
spiritual, and be eager and willing to share
Your love for them, just as You have bestowed
Your love upon us.

Independence

DAY 15

★
★★

*This I pray, that your love may abound
still more and more in knowledge and all
discernment, that you may approve the things
that are excellent, that you may be sincere and
without offense till the day of Christ.*

PHILIPPIANS 1:9–10

Father,
May Your love flow through and around us.
Speak to our hearts and open our minds that
we may see You and the light of Your glory.
Cleanse us, O Lord, that we may stand before
You without blemish. Help us as a nation to
be a discerning people with moral voices who
bring honor and glory to You, O God.

Abraham Lincoln

Fondly do we hope—fervently do we pray—that this mighty scourge of war may speedily pass away. Yet, if God wills that it continue . . . until every drop of blood drawn with the lash shall be paid by another drawn with the sword . . . so still it must be said "the judgments of the Lord are true and righteous altogether." With malice toward none; with charity for all; with firmness in the right, as God gives us to see the right, let us strive on to finish the work we are in; to bind up the nation's wounds; to care for him who shall have borne the battle, and for his widow and his orphan, to do all which may achieve and cherish a just and a lasting peace among ourselves and with all nations.

—Second Inaugural
Address, March 4, 1865

DAY 16

I bow my knees to the Father of our Lord Jesus Christ, from whom the whole family in heaven and earth is named, that He would grant you, according to the riches of His glory, to be strengthened with might through His Spirit in the inner man . . . to know the love of Christ which passes knowledge; that you may be filled with all the fullness of God.

EPHESIANS 3:14–16, 19

Lord,

We bow before You in humble thanksgiving for Your gifts of power and strength, fortitude and might! We claim the riches of Your glory and the fullness of Your grace that come through the indwelling of Your Spirit within us. We pray for our nation to remain firm and steadfast in the knowledge of Your truth and the promise of the victory that is ours through Christ, who loves us.

I will sing to the LORD as long as I live;
I will sing praise to my God while I have
   my being.
May my meditation be sweet to Him;
I will be glad in the LORD.

PSALM 104:33–34

O Lord,
We lift our voices and praise Your holy name!
May You forever be the center of our thoughts,
that in all things we may lift You up in worship and song. Let the words of our mouths
and the meditations of our hearts be a sweet
aroma to You, for You are our King—our joy
comes from You! Righteousness and justice
are the foundation of Your throne; therefore,
we praise Your holy name forever.

Independence

DAY 18

★
★★

Give ear to my words, O Lord,
Consider my meditation.
Give heed to the voice of my cry,
My King and my God,
For to You I will pray.
My voice You shall hear in the morning, O Lord;
In the morning I will direct it to You,
And I will look up.

PSALM 5:1–3

O Lord,
We beg You to hear our supplications. Do not let our words fall on deaf ears. Let us come to You each morning with hearts full of joy, for You are our Most High God, and everything we have comes from You. Bless us that we might bless others. Let us always look to You for every provision. Let us each be an open vessel filled with Your wisdom, that others might know Your saving grace.

Hear me when I call, O God of my
righteousness!
You have relieved me in my distress;
Have mercy on me, and hear my prayer.

PSALM 4:1

Father,
You are *so* wonderful! Through Jesus Christ
we have an open invitation to come to You in
prayer. We give thanks for this blessing and
each day find joy in all that You give to us.
What a blessed people we are to know and
embrace Your unconditional love.

Independence

DAY 20

★
★ ★

The Lord has heard my supplication;
The Lord will receive my prayer.

PSALM 6:9

Father,
We thank You for hearing our petition.
Strengthen us by the power of Your Spirit to
live in such a way that glorifies You. Forgive
us when we do things that displease You and
separate us from Your presence. Lead us each
day, that we might live lives that are pleasing
to You. May You forever be praised.

FRANKLIN D. ROOSEVELT

Almighty God: Our sons, pride of our nation, this day have set upon a mighty endeavor, a struggle to preserve our Republic, our religion, and our civilization, and to set free a suffering humanity.

Lead them straight and true; give strength to their arms, stoutness to their hearts, steadfastness in their faith. . . . Their road will be long and hard. For the enemy is strong. . . . Success may not come with rushing speed, but we shall return again and again; and we know by Thy grace, and by the righteousness of our cause, our sons will triumph. . . .

With Thy blessing, we shall prevail over the unholy forces of our enemy. Help us to conquer the apostles of greed and racial arrogances. Lead us to the saving of our country, and with our sister nations into a world unity that will spell a sure peace—a peace invulnerable to the schemings of unworthy men. And a peace that will let all men live in freedom, reaping the just rewards of their honest toil.

—D-DAY, JUNE 6, 1944

DAY 21

★
★ ★

Because Your lovingkindness is better than life,
My lips shall praise You.
Thus I will bless You while I live;
I will lift up my hands in Your name. . . .
Because You have been my help,
Therefore in the shadow of Your wings
*   I will rejoice.*

PSALM 63:3–4, 7

Lord,

We praise You for Your grace, mercy, and
lovingkindness. May we as a nation look to
You with thanksgiving in our hearts for the
blessings You have poured upon us. Let us
forever rest in the shadow of Your wings and
shout for joy with praise, for You are a most
gracious God, and You bless us even beyond
our understanding.

DAY 22

★
★ ★

Hear my cry, O God;
Attend to my prayer.
From the end of the earth I will cry to You,
When my heart is overwhelmed;
Lead me to the rock that is higher than I.
For You have been a shelter for me,
A strong tower from the enemy.
I will abide in Your tabernacle forever;
I will trust in the shelter of Your wings.

PSALM 61:1–4

Father,

We recognize that there are those who would speak evil against You when hardship knocks at their door. Let us forever stand firm in the foundation of our faith. Let us live in the center of Your will. We will come to You each day for strength and endurance. Help us, O God, to be the people You wish us to be, for we trust in You.

Independence

DAY 23

You, O my God, have revealed to Your servant
that You will build him a house. Therefore Your
servant has found it in his heart to pray before You.
And now, LORD, You are God, and have promised
this goodness to Your servant. Now You have been
pleased to bless the house of Your servant, that
it may continue before You forever; for You have
blessed it, O LORD, and it shall be blessed forever.

1 CHRONICLES 17:25–27

Lord,

We are so blessed that each day You come
to us with the gift of Your Spirit to help us
and strengthen our purpose for Your glory.
Continue to work in us, and help us grow to
be the people You wish us to be. Thank You
for Your continued goodness even when we
stumble. Your unconditional love has been
promised forever. Thank You for Your gracious mercy to us each day.

*"Whatever things you ask when you pray,
believe that you receive them, and you will have
them. And whenever you stand praying, if you
have anything against anyone, forgive him,
that your Father in heaven may also forgive you
your trespasses."*

MARK 11:24–25

Father,

Help our nation with its unbelief! Lead us
into a renewed relationship with You! Forgive
us when we find fault in our brothers. Help
us look beyond their shortcomings and look
deeper within ourselves to become better
people. Forgive us when we fall short of doing
all that You've called us to do, and when
we fail to demonstrate love and forgiveness
toward those who wrong us. Thank You for
the blessing of knowing that we are for-
given—no matter what.

33

Independence

DAY 25

*Now it came to pass, as He was praying in a
certain place, when He ceased, that one of His
disciples said to Him, "Lord, teach us to pray, as
John also taught his disciples."*

LUKE 11:1

Lord,
We come to You with open hearts and ask
that You speak to our spirits with words of
wisdom and direction, that we may know
how You wish for us to pray. Help Your
humble servants to speak words of praise and
adoration, for You are the King of kings and
the Lord of lords. Teach us, Lord, that we may
know You and the power of Your resurrection. Fill us with Your presence and forgive
our shortcomings. Lead us, O Lord, to a
higher place, that You might be lifted up and
draw all men to You.

JOHN F. KENNEDY

Let us therefore proclaim our gratitude to Providence for manifold blessings—let us be humbly thankful for inherited ideals—and let us resolve to share those blessings and those ideals with our fellow human beings throughout the world. . . .

On that day let us gather in sanctuaries dedicated to worship and in homes blessed by family affection to express our gratitude for the glorious gifts of God; and let us earnestly and humbly pray that He will continue to guide and sustain us in the great unfinished tasks of achieving peace, justice, and understanding among all men and nations and of ending misery and suffering wherever they exist.

—WRITTEN FOR
THANKSGIVING DAY 1963

DAY 26

★
★ ★

Give ear to my prayer, O God,
And do not hide Yourself from my supplication.
Attend to me, and hear me;
I am restless in my complaint, and moan
     noisily.

PSALM 55:1–2

Lord,
There are so many times when we have burdens almost too heavy to bear. Our nation faces hardships and pain; we need Your wisdom and help in all areas. Strengthen us as a people and lead us in the way that will bring honor and glory to You. Lord, You have promised that if we humble ourselves and seek Your face and pray, You will heal our land. May we forever be humble in Your sight, and may we experience Your blessings in the midst of our great need.

Cast your burden on the LORD,
And He shall sustain you;
He shall never permit the righteous to
  be moved.

PSALM 55:22

Lord,
You are so wonderful. Thank You for caring about our burdens. Open our hearts to Your Spirit and let us listen to Your voice. Strengthen us, O God, with confidence in You, that we may live for You and glorify Your name. Father, we praise You for all the gifts that You have given us. Draw us close to You that we may see Your glory.

Independence

DAY 28

The mouth of the righteous speaks wisdom,
And his tongue talks of justice.
The law of his God is in his heart;
None of his steps shall slide.

PSALM 37:30–31

Father,
True wisdom is a gift that only You, Lord, can give. May we always be in right standing with You. Let the words we speak honor You, and let us never speak Your name in vain. Let us stay steadfast and live in such a way that Your light will shine through us wherever we go. Thank You, Father, for Your mercy and love.

*Jesus answered and said to [His disciples],
"Assuredly, I say to you, if you have faith and
do not doubt, you will not only do what was
done to the fig tree, but also if you say to this
mountain, 'Be removed and be cast into the
sea,' it will be done. And whatever things you
ask in prayer, believing, you will receive."*

MATTHEW 21:21–22

O Lord,
Strengthen our faith. Help us never to doubt
Your Word or Your faithfulness. Lift us up
that we may boldly proclaim Your truth each
and every day. Let us be sensitive to the leading of Your Spirit and never forget that "I can
do all things through Christ who strengthens
me" (Philippians 4:13). Lord, we praise You
because Your mercies are new every morning
and Your faithfulness is great.

Independence

DAY 30

I exhort first of all that supplications, prayers, intercessions, and giving of thanks be made for all men, for kings and all who are in authority, that we may lead a quiet and peaceable life in all godliness and reverence. For this is good and acceptable in the sight of God our Savior.

1 TIMOTHY 2:1–3

Lord,

Our nation needs Your guidance and direction. We humbly ask that Your Spirit intercede with the leaders of the nation, giving them the wisdom to make decisions that will honor You. We pray fervently for peace both here and abroad. Let us live with reverence for You and with peace in our hearts for our fellow man. We know this is Your desire. May we always remember that You are our God and Savior.

Ronald Reagan

To preserve our blessed land we must look to God. . . . It is time to realize that we need God more than He needs us. . . .

Let us, young and old, join together, as did the First Continental Congress, in the first step—in humble heartfelt prayer. Let us do so for the love of God and His great goodness, in search of His guidance and the grace of repentance, in seeking His blessings, His peace, and the resting of His kind and holy hands on ourselves, our nation, our friends in the defense of freedom, and all mankind, now and always.

The time has come to turn to God and reassert our trust in Him for the healing of America. . . . Our country is in need of and ready for a spiritual renewal. Today, we utter no prayer more fervently than the ancient prayer for peace on earth.

"The LORD bless you and keep you; the LORD make His face shine upon you, and be gracious unto you; the LORD lift up His countenance upon you, and give you peace." And God bless you all.

—FROM A SPEECH TO THE AMERICAN PEOPLE,

FEBRUARY 6, 1986

Because Your lovingkindness is better than life,
My lips shall praise You.
Thus I will bless You while I live;
I will lift up my hands in Your name.
My soul shall be satisfied as with marrow
  and fatness,
And my mouth shall praise You with joyful lips.

PSALM 63:3–5

O Lord,
Let us never forget to praise Your holy name.
You are a wonderful God. You are slow to
anger and patient, with an unconditional love
that has no end. Let us bless You each day and
lift up our thanks in praise for the wonderful
things You have done for us. May we forever
give honor to Your name, for without You we
are nothing.

Independence

DAY 32

★
★ ★

This Book of the Law shall not depart from your mouth, but you shall meditate in it day and night, that you may observe to do according to all that is written in it. For then you will make your way prosperous, and then you will have good success.

JOSHUA 1:8

Father,

You have given us a guide for life and have asked us to meditate in Your Word day and night. Place that desire within our hearts— give us a hunger for Your Word, that we may know You. Lord, You want us to be successful in life and to be prosperous in all that we do. Lead us back to Your Word that we may honor You through all that we say and do.

How precious is Your lovingkindness, O God!
Therefore the children of men put their trust
  under the shadow of Your wings.
They are abundantly satisfied with the fullness
  of Your house,
And You give them drink from the river of Your
  pleasures.
For with You is the fountain of life;
In Your light we see light.

                                    PSALM 36:7–9

Lord,
Your lovingkindness is new every day. May
we forever trust in You with all our hearts and
find rest in the shelter of Your love. The very
life we live comes from You alone. Bless us, O
Lord, with the light of Your presence and place
within us the desire to share Your light so that
others may come to know the saving grace of
our Lord and Savior.

Independence

DAY 34

★
★ ★

The LORD is my light and my salvation;
Whom shall I fear?
The LORD is the strength of my life;
Of whom shall I be afraid?

PSALM 27:1

O Lord,
Today we face many hardships in a time when
our faith is continually tested. But we know
there is nothing to fear because You, Lord, are
in control of all things. You are our Strength
and our Defender; there is nothing too hard
for You. Therefore, let us be confident in
our faith and bold in telling others of Your
marvelous unconditional love.

I will bless the LORD at all times;
His praise shall continually be in my mouth. . . .
Oh, magnify the LORD with me,
And let us exalt His name together.

PSALM 34:1, 3

Lord,
You are the Creator of the universe—we praise
Your blessed and holy name! You alone are the
provider of all things, and with You all things
are possible—may You always be lifted up!
Let us live each day in the center of Your will
and live for Your glory. If we say nothing, the
rocks will cry out Your magnificent name. Let
all men praise Your holy name, for You are a
marvelous God, and Your light shines over all
who choose to call You Lord.

Independence

Dwight D. Eisenhower

Almighty God, as we stand here at this moment my future associates in the executive branch of government join me in beseeching that Thou will make full and complete our dedication to the service of the people in this throng, and their fellow citizens everywhere.

Give us, we pray, the power to discern clearly right from wrong, and allow all our words and actions to be governed thereby, and by the laws of this land. Especially we pray that our concern shall be for all the people regardless of station, race, or calling.

May cooperation be permitted and be the mutual aim of those who, under the concepts of our Constitution, hold to differing political faiths; so that all may work for the good of our beloved country and Thy glory. Amen.

—FIRST ACT AFTER RECEIVING THE OATH OF OFFICE, JANUARY 20, 1953

Teach me Your way, O LORD;
I will walk in Your truth;
Unite my heart to fear Your name.
I will praise You, O Lord my God, with all my
    heart,
And I will glorify Your name forevermore.

PSALM 86:11–12

Lord,

We hunger for Your Word. Teach us the way that we should go, and help us walk in Your truth each day. May Your praise always be on our lips, and may You fill our hearts with the joy of Your love and blessing. You are a gracious and loving God whose mercy is new every morning.

Independence

DAY 37

*I will bless the L*ORD *who has given me counsel;*
My heart also instructs me in the night seasons.
*I have set the L*ORD *always before me;*
Because He is at my right hand I shall not
   be moved.

PSALM 16:7–8

Father,
We humbly ask for Your blessing. Help us to
listen to Your counsel when we are alone with
You. Speak to our hearts each moment, for
You are the anchor of our souls, and we will
rest in Your presence. It is You alone we desire,
and no one or nothing can take Your place.

Blessed is the man
Who walks not in the counsel of the ungodly,
 Nor stands in the path of sinners,
 Nor sits in the seat of the scornful;
But his delight is in the law of the LORD,
 And in His law he meditates day and
  night.

PSALM 1:1–2

Lord,
Your Word has given us counsel on how we should relate to and act toward one another. May we be steadfast and immovable in our commitment to You and to one another. Let our roots go deep into Your Word to praise and glorify Your name. May our weakness be Your strength and our purpose in life be to honor You.

Independence

DAY 39

★
★★

Hear a just cause, O Lord,
Attend to my cry;
Give ear to my prayer which is not from deceitful
lips. . . .
Let Your eyes look on the things that are
upright. . . .
That my footsteps may not slip.

PSALM 17:1–2, 5

Lord,
We cry out to You with hearts that need Your
blessings. Give us wisdom to make the right
decisions that will bring honor to You and
will purify our hearts. Let the words that we
speak draw us closer to Your presence. We
recognize, O Lord, that You are in control of
all things. Help this nation to hear Your voice,
protect us from evil, and lead us in the path
of righteousness for Your name's sake.

★
★ ★

Let every soul be subject to the governing authorities. For there is no authority except from God, and the authorities that exist are appointed by God. . . . Render therefore to all their due: taxes to whom taxes are due, customs to whom customs, fear to whom fear, honor to whom honor.

ROMANS 13:1, 7

Lord,
We live in a nation that is free to elect those chosen for public office. We confess that the servants who are chosen are there with Your approval. Let us faithfully support those elected to office, giving honor to their position. Let us help them fulfill the obligation and responsibility for our nation. With prayer and understanding, let us unite ourselves to the one purpose of living a life in which "In God We Trust."

Independence

PSALM 119:33–40

Teach me, O LORD, the way of Your statutes,
And I shall keep it to the end.
Give me understanding, and I shall keep
     Your law;
Indeed, I shall observe it with my whole heart.
Make me walk in the path of Your
     commandments,
For I delight in it.
Incline my heart to Your testimonies,
And not to covetousness.
Turn away my eyes from looking at
     worthless things,
And revive me in Your way.
Establish Your word to Your servant,
Who is devoted to fearing You.
Turn away my reproach which I dread,
For Your judgments are good.
Behold, I long for Your precepts;
Revive me in Your righteousness.

We the People

... a domestic Tranquility, provide for the common ...
... our Posterity, do ordain and establish this C...

... tion. 1. All legislative Powers herein gran...
Representatives.

... tion. 2. The House of Representatives sha...
... ach State shall have the Qualifications requisite for ...

No Person shall be a Repres...
... cake shall not, when elected, be ...

Representatives and direct ...
... embers, which shall be determin...
... taxed, three fifths of all other ...
... nd within every subsequen...
... rty thousand, but each s...
... ntitled to chuse three, M...
... right, Delaware one, M...
When vacancies hap...
... the House of Rep...

Section. 3. The Senate ...
... Senator shall have one Vote.

THE GREAT AWAKENINGS

THE FIRST GREAT AWAKENING

The Great Awakening was a period (1734–45) in our history when revival spread throughout the colonies and people were drawn to prayer and a greater spiritual experience. This was a time when American colonies were questioning the role of the individual in their Christian walk and their role in society. This was a time of enlightenment, which emphasized the power of each individual to understand the approach to salvation and the power of prayer.

Great men such as Jonathan Edwards and George Whitefield were key Americans who preached for close to ten years in New England colonies with an emphasis on the personal approach to religion. These men helped unify the American colonies and helped the Great Awakening spread through the work of numerous preachers and revivals. This movement fulfilled people's need for reassurance, direction, and religious purpose. People became united in the understanding of their Christian faith and life.

Jonathan Edwards

THE SECOND GREAT AWAKENING

The Second Great Awaken-
ing was a Christian
revival movement during the
early nineteenth century in
the United States. It began
around 1800 and gained
momentum by 1820. The
movement expressed a
theology, by which every
person could be saved through
revivals.

Many converts believed that the awakening heralded a new millennial age. This
awakening stimulated the establishment of
many reform movements designed to remedy
the evils of society before the second coming of
Jesus Christ.

During this time in history, church membership soared. The Methodist circuit riders
and local Baptist preachers made enormous

gains. In the newly settled frontier regions, the revival was implemented through camp meetings. Each camp meeting was a religious service of several days' length with multiple preachers. They were committed to individuals achieving a personal relationship with Jesus Christ.

The Second Great Awakening had a profound impact on American religious history. The membership numbers of the Baptist and Methodists grew dramatically during this period in history. The application of Christian teaching to social problems was commonplace during the early part of the nineteenth century.*

---

*https://www.christianity.com/church/church-history/%20timeline/1701-1800/the-great-awakening-11630212.html

Camp Meeting of the Methodists N America

THE THIRD GREAT AWAKENING

During the Third Great Awakening, religion played a dominant role in American history. Protestant denominations had a strong sense of social activism. They developed the postmillennial theology that the second coming of Christ would come after the entire earth had been reformed. Social issues gained momentum from the awakening, as did the worldwide missionary movement.

This was a time in history that the mainline Protestant churches were rapidly increasing in number. As the numbers grew, so did their wealth and educational levels. Focusing on reaching the unchurched in America and around the world, many built colleges and universities to train the next generation. In society, the role of a missionary was held in high regard.

Charles Finney